AF510104

INTERNAL AFFAIRS

INTERNAL AFFAIRS

Alioune Sow

Contents

Copyright © 2025 by Alioune Sow
All rights reserved. No part of this book may be reproduced in any manner whatsoever without written permission except in the case of brief quotations embodied in critical articles and reviews.
First Printing, 2025

Above all, the author extends profound gratitude to his steadfast collaborators, mentors, and those who supported him throughout this journey, as well as the unseen guiding presence he credits for his perseverance.

Alioune Sow humbly acknowledges that he is not a business expert but rather an entrepreneur shaped by lived experience. This work reflects lessons learned, challenges navigated, and insights forged through trial, error, and an unwavering commitment to his core values.

With the author's consent, this book documents Alioune Sow's journey as an entrepreneur and his resilience in navigating systemic obstacles, including his entanglement with—and triumph over—the criminal justice system.

Finally, he leaves readers with a guiding principle, inspired by physicist Richard Feynman's wisdom on embracing the unfamiliar:

"Things on a very small scale behave like nothing you have any direct experience with... They do not behave like waves, particles, clouds, billiard balls, weights on springs, or anything you have ever seen."

1

From Incarceration to Illumination

Like many entrepreneurs, Alioune Sow's journey is a mosaic of borrowed wisdom and hard-earned lessons. His path began not with a grand vision, but with quiet observation—studying the stumbles of others to avoid their pitfalls. Early in his career, he watched a mentor's tech startup collapse under the weight of rapid scaling without customer validation. This lesson became foundational: Growth without purpose is a house built on sand. Today, his ventures—a misunderstood community initiative aimed at bridging digital literacy gaps in rural West Africa and a fledgling clothing brand celebrating Afrocentric artistry—remain dormant, their potential veiled by public ambiguity. Yet Alioune sees this not as failure, but as a chrysalis stage, a necessary pause to recalibrate.

Alioune attributes this stagnation to his early navigation of capitalist frameworks, where financial acumen often overshadows human-centric values. In his youth, he viewed profit as the ultimate scorecard. Now, he redefines money as a "kinetic currency"—a tool for energy exchange that amplifies impact, outpaces competition, and anticipates seismic market shifts. As both founder and spiritual counselor, he stitches together disparate perspectives: the communal Sabr (patience) of Senegal's Wolof people, who endure hardship with grace, and the relentless innovation of Silicon Valley. His growth mirrors a marathoner's discipline: incremental, intentional, and rooted in clarity.

Embracing Failure as Fertile Ground

While statistics coldly declare that 60% of startups fail within their first decade, Alioune reframes these odds as a call to arms. For niche entrepreneurs, he argues, failure is not an endpoint but a diagnostic tool—a chance to dissect what went wrong and engineer a smarter pivot. Consider the rebirth of Slack, which evolved from a failed gaming venture into a $27B collaboration empire. Alioune's own rebranding philosophy hinges on research-driven reinvention: mining setbacks for insights, then aligning offerings with unmet needs.

His vision transcends profit. Drawing from his upbringing in a Senegalese village where community well-being trumped individual gain, he champions mental health advocacy as a business imperative. In a world where burnout is a badge of honor, Alioune's ventures will integrate "resilience hubs"—digital platforms offering free therapy resources and peer support networks, blending Afrocentric wisdom with modern psychology.

The iPhone Epiphany: Bridging Continents Through "Spiritual Alchemy"

A decade ago, while bartering smartphones in a Lagos market, Alioune had an epiphany: the same device that fueled distraction in the West could democratize education in Africa. Inspired by Steve Jobs' fusion of art and technology, he now asks: How might mobile tools ignite a renaissance across underserved regions? His answer lies in "spiritual alchemy"—a synergy of persistence, contextual intelligence, and culturally rooted innovation.

For instance, he envisions an app merging oral storytelling traditions with AI-driven literacy tools, preserving indigenous languages while equipping users with coding skills. Education, to Alioune, is the great equalizer—but only if it honors local heritage. "You can't copy-paste Silicon Valley into Dakar," he insists. "True disruption respects roots."

Emotional Intelligence: The Invisible Infrastructure of Leadership

Alioune champions emotional intelligence (EQ) as the bedrock of sustainable success. During a heated boardroom clash over budget cuts, he defused tension by shifting focus from spreadsheets to shared values: What legacy do we want this decision to reflect? This moment crystallized his belief that EQ is a "magnetic force"—a blend of self-awareness, empathy, and regulation that transforms conflicts into collaborations.

He practices "micro-acts of empathy": handwritten notes to disgruntled customers, flexible deadlines for stressed teams. These gestures, small but systemic, ripple through his ventures. His North Star? Bhutan's Gross National Happiness Index—a reminder that societies thriving beyond GDP prioritize holistic well-being.

Rebranding Through Spiritual Anchors: The Incarceration Crucible

Currently incarcerated in Ohio, Alioune has turned confinement into a laboratory for renewal. Each morning, he meditates on a single question: Does this action nourish my spirit or feed my ego? This practice, born of necessity, has clarified why his early ventures faltered—they prioritized scale over soul.

His "Open 64" framework—a compass spanning spiritual, cultural, and financial domains—structures his days. Mondays focus on mental agility (chess strategy, coding tutorials), Tuesdays on community connection (letters to aspiring entrepreneurs). Rebranding, to him, is akin to retrofitting a vintage car: preserving its essence while upgrading its engine.

Legacy and the Long Game: Soccer, Systems, and Soul

A lifelong soccer enthusiast, Alioune draws parallels between teamwork and business ecosystems. He cites FC Barcelona's tiki-taka style—a symphony of short passes and spatial awareness—as a metaphor for agile leadership. "Success isn't about solo brilliance," he notes. "It's about designing systems where every pass matters."

His metric for impact? Depth over reach. Whether mentoring a single inmate in business basics or launching a continent-wide digital platform, he measures success by lives recalibrated, not revenue generated.

From Incarceration to Inspiration: The Alchemy of Adversity

Behind bars, Alioune has authored a manifesto marrying Napoleon Hill's Think and Grow Rich with Senegalese proverbs. Each chapter ends with a "rebellion prompt"—e.g., Identify one rule you've mindlessly obeyed. How might bending it spark innovation? His mantra: True treasure isn't mined from the earth but cultivated in communities.

As Malcolm Forbes once warned, "Bulky empires crumble; agile ideals endure." For Alioune, rebranding is more than a tactic—it's a testament to the human spirit's capacity to rewrite narratives. From a cell in Ohio, he's proof that even the darkest soil can nurture seeds of transformation.

Final Word

Alioune Sow's story is a beacon for the disenfranchised and a blueprint for the visionary. In a world obsessed with speed, he offers a radical counter-narrative: Sometimes, to move forward, you must first plant your feet in the soil of your roots. His journey reminds us that the most profound revolutions begin not with a roar, but with a whisper—a quiet resolve to rebuild, rebrand, and rise.

2

Redefining the Ecosystem

Labeling Alioune Sow's ventures as mere "products" undersells their complexity. While Merriam-Webster defines an ecosystem as "a community of organisms interacting with their environment," Alioune's vision transcends industrial frameworks. His ecosystem operates like a wellness retreat—a dynamic, interconnected space blending innovation, culture, and sustainability.

Evolution as a Business Imperative

In a world where outdated technology is swiftly replaced, Alioune views products as tools to solve problems or enhance efficiency. His favorites? Software solutions that marry intuitive design with productivity gains. This philosophy drives his rebranding mission: to elevate his ecosystem from stagnation to global relevance by addressing past shortcomings.

The Re-branding Blueprint: From Diagnosis to Renaissance

Alioune's first ventures faltered due to intuition-led decisions and scant planning. Now, he prioritizes data-driven strategies and "shadow work"—pre-launch research to uncover blind spots and competitive edges. Think of it as an incubation period: drafting frameworks, stress-testing ideas, and aligning values with market demands.

Core Entities in the Ecosystem

The Millennial Partners Group

Vision: A think tank fostering innovation through collaboration.

Roadmap:

2025: Rebrand for modern relevance

2026: Expand market reach

2027: Pioneer digital solutions

2028: Cement thought leadership

Fountanké Industries

Vision: A tribal conglomerate promoting entrepreneurship.

Roadmap:

2025: Rebrand for clarity

2026: Strengthen operations

2027: Accelerate product innovation

2028: Forge strategic alliances

Why Rebrand?

Declining impact, shifting industries, and unfulfilled potential necessitate a renaissance. Alioune's goal: transform his ecosystem into a cohesive, value-driven network that thrives even in his absence.

The Ten Dimensions of Ecosystem Success

Alioune's ecosystem rests on ten pillars:

1. Familiar (cultural roots)
2. Financial (sustainability)
3. Emotional (EQ-driven leadership)
4. Impact (measurable change)
5. Social (community engagement)
6. Physical (operational infrastructure)
7. Environmental (sustainable practices)
8. Intellectual (innovation)
9. Career (growth opportunities)
10. Leisure (work-life balance)

These dimensions ensure holistic growth, blending prosperity with purpose.

Execution: From Vision to Reality

Phase 1 (90 Days):

Graphic Design & Branding: Modernize logos, colors, and symbols to reflect core values.

Audience Research: Conduct surveys to align rebranding with community expectations (e.g., integrating charity work).

Phase 2:

R&D + Fundraising: Develop a virtual-first ecosystem to maximize reach with minimal budget.

Team Assembly: Recruit freelancers and vision-aligned talent to drive execution.

Phase 3 (9-Month Launch):

Simplify engagement, amplify awareness, and measure success through KPIs like audience growth and solution velocity.

Philosophy Meets Pragmatism, Cooperative Model Over Independence

Alioune shifts from solo entrepreneurship to a cooperative framework, fostering creativity and resilience. This model thrives on:

Reverse Mentorship: Junior members lead in emerging fields like blockchain.

Balanced Culture: Prioritizing peace and harmony to preempt disruptions.

Combatting Distractions

A visual tool—three concentric circles (self, team, ecosystem)—keeps focus on incremental progress. As Alioune notes, "Progress is a skill—one I aim to master."

The Irony of Incarceration: A Catalyst for Clarity

Despite his circumstances, Alioune leverages solitude to refine strategies. He views himself as a "medium for inspiration," channeling setbacks into fuel for innovation. His mantra: "Failure is not an option in rebranding—only evolution."

Conclusion: The View from the Valley

Rebranding isn't just a facelift—it's a movement. For Alioune, it's about aligning with Chesterton's wisdom: "One sees great things from the valley, only small things from the peak." By embracing humility, creativity, and tenacity, his ecosystem aims to redefine success, proving that even from confinement, one can illuminate paths for generations.

3

The Architecture of Success

Organization is the silent orchestrator of progress—a meticulously choreographed interplay of ideas, resources, and intent that transforms chaos into coherence. Just as Earth's ecosystems avoid collapse through symbiotic relationships and responsible waste cycles, businesses thrive by adopting a similar ethos of balance. Take IKEA's inventory management system, which uses AI to predict regional demand spikes, or Tesla's safeguards around its battery patents, which protect intellectual property while fostering industry-wide innovation. Effective placement transcends mere logistics; it is a strategic ballet where visibility and security perform in tandem. Consider Amazon's algorithmic pricing—its real-time adjustments shield against competitors while ensuring products remain discoverable to millions. This dance is not just about survival but about creating value that endures.

The Global Challenge: Bridging Markets, Cultures, and Habits

Expanding into international markets demands more than translated slogans—it requires cultural fluency. In Japan, Starbucks reimagined its stores as "third places" for relaxation, introducing matcha lattes and tatami seating to align with local rituals. Alioune's ecosystem faces a parallel challenge: resonating with Francophone West Africa's communal values while engaging the global Pan-African diaspora's hunger for cultural reconnection.

Cultural Nuances in Practice:

Francophone West Africa: A region where oral traditions dictate trust-building. Alioune's initiatives might integrate griot storytelling into digital platforms, blending ancestral wisdom with fintech solutions.

Pan-African Diaspora: Communities in the U.S. and Europe seeking roots. Collaborations with artists like Burna Boy or Afropop festivals could anchor his clothing brand in cultural pride.

Digital Natives: Gen Z's demand for instant gratification is met through TikTok campaigns showcasing real-time impact—e.g., a live stream of artisans crafting garments in Dakar.

Data acts as a compass here. The U.S. Census reveals that 46% of African immigrants hold bachelor's degrees—a statistic Alioune might leverage to tailor educational tech tools for diaspora professionals.

Market Dominance: The Art of War in Business

Market dominance is a chess game where offensive creativity and defensive vigilance coexist.

Offensive Tactics:

Curiosity-Driven Campaigns: Mimicking Liquid Death's viral marketing, which turned water into a "punk" beverage, Alioune could repurpose competitor slogans. Imagine a billboard in Lagos reading: "While Others Talk Heritage, We Live It."

Psychological Positioning: Apple's "Think Different" ethos isn't about specs—it's about identity. Alioune's brands might anchor messaging in Afro-futurism, positioning products as keys to a reimagined African renaissance.

Defensive Posture:

Agile Pivots: When Netflix noticed password-sharing erosion, it launched "Profiles" to monetize the trend. Similarly, Alioune could convert bootlegged tribal designs into licensed collaborations, turning pirates into partners.

Case in Point: David vs. Goliath Revisited

Goliath's mythical nearsightedness mirrors corporate blind spots. Kodak's dismissal of digital photography, despite inventing it, allowed startups like Canon to dominate. Alioune's playbook? Exploit legacy competitors' inertia. For instance, while global banks overlook West Africa's unbanked population, his ecosystem could deploy blockchain-powered microfinance apps, leveraging local susu (savings circle) traditions.

Digital Imperatives: The Velocity of Trust

In an era where 53% of mobile users abandon sites taking longer than three seconds to load, digital friction is a silent killer.

Seamless UX in Action:

Speed: Shopify's one-click checkout boosted conversions by 50%. Alioune's platforms might adopt voice-to-pay tech, reducing steps for users with limited literacy.

Simplicity: Duolingo's gamified interface, which turned language learning into a habit, could inspire Alioune's educational tools.

Social-First Community Building:
Instagram's "Shop Tab" isn't just a feature—it's a cultural hub. Alioune's one-page landings for Fountanké Industries might embed TikTok-style DIY videos, teaching sustainable dyeing techniques while subtly marketing kits.

Customer Service: The Loyalty Lifeline

Good Service: Zappos' 365-day returns and surprise upgrades birthed cult loyalty. Alioune's "Community Custodians" program could offer real-time WhatsApp support in local dialects.

Bad Service: United Airlines' $1.4 billion stock plunge after a passenger-dragging incident underscores reputational fragility. Proactive empathy audits might preempt such crises.

Metrics That Matter: The Pulse of Progress
Rebranding without data is like sailing without stars.

Key Metrics:

Web Traffic: Tools like Hotjar map user journeys, revealing friction points. A spike in Nigerian mobile traffic might prompt a Yoruba-language interface.

Conversion Rates: A/B testing landing pages with Afrobeats playlists vs. silent designs could reveal cultural triggers.

Resource Efficiency: Toyota's "Just-in-Time" model, which slashed warehouse costs, inspires lean inventory tactics for Alioune's artisan partners.

The Feedback Loop:
Surveys are diagnostic tools. When Slack noticed user frustration with email overload, it pivoted from a gaming platform to a communication hub—a lesson in listening.

The Virtual Ecosystem: A Bridge to Legacy
Alioune's virtual ecosystem is both mirror and mold—reflecting cultural roots while shaping future economies.

Geographical Clusters:
In Accra, a digital hub could connect shea butter cooperatives with eco-beauty startups like Liha, using AR to showcase sourcing journeys.

Reverse Mentorship:
At IBM, junior staff teach executives blockchain basics. Alioune's ecosystem might pair Senegalese coders with Silicon Valley veterans, blending ancestral problem-solving with tech rigor.

Value-Aligned Partnerships:

Patagonia's "1% for the Planet" model—donating profits to eco-causes—could inspire Alioune's collaborations with groups like AfroCharts, streaming music to fund literacy apps.

Conclusion: The Infinite Balance

As Dajan Stojanovic poetically notes, "There is a pledge of the big and of the small in the infinite." For Alioune, placement is the alchemy of scale and specificity—a Ghanaian cocoa farmer's story shared in a Brooklyn pop-up, or a Wolof proverb encoded in a Nairobi app's UX. By marrying Silicon Valley's agility with Ubuntu's communal ethos, his ecosystem doesn't just compete—it redefines the rules, proving that true progress lies not in dominance, but in harmony.

4

Foundations of Business Value and Pricing

A business's value is shaped by its financial health, growth potential, internal dynamics, and operational efficiency. Pricing strategies hinge on production costs and profit margins, fluctuating with market demand and supply constraints. While traditional businesses focus on profitability, nonprofits innovate to secure funding through community engagement and superior service. Allen redefines price as "the intersection of product affordability and the problem it solves," emphasizing competitive relevance.

2. The Perception Gap: A Study on Value

A New York University study revealed a striking disconnect: only 17% of participants (ages 21–45 with college education) could define "value," and a mere 7% articulated their personal value clearly. This underscores the need for businesses to educate consumers on their offerings' worth, bridging the gap between perception and reality.

3. Strategic Pricing and Marketing in the Digital Age

Pricing communicates brand positioning and quality. Practice-based pricing—starting low and scaling with customer loyalty—can align with audience growth. Marketing success lies in emphasizing four value pillars:

1. Functional (utility)
2. Inventory (scarcity)
3. Social (community impact)
4. Psychological (emotional resonance)

Collaborations with influencers and leveraging social media amplify reach, even with limited budgets, by tapping into pre-existing audiences.

4. Real Estate Pricing: Beyond Bricks and Mortar

In real estate, pricing reflects neighborhood averages, community amenities, and property conditions. External factors like market trends and competitor activity also play pivotal roles, illustrating that pricing transcends mere cost calculations.

5. Metrics That Matter: KPIs for Growth

Critical KPIs include investment returns, revenue streams, and profit margins. Operational efficiency is gauged through product availability, delivery speed, and customer satisfaction. For Alioune's ecosystem, priorities are:

1. Audience engagement
2. Brand visibility
3. Task automation
4. Market expansion

6. The Human Element in an Automated World

Despite assumptions of AI dominance, thriving companies maintain simplicity and human-centric operations. Direct customer engagement and efficient service delivery remain irreplaceable.

7. Alioune's Vision: An Afrocentric Ecosystem

Alioune's ecosystem blends cultural pride with value-driven solutions, prioritizing community over profit. Initiatives like Project Gamora (Millennial Partners Group) and the Community Reserve (Fountanké Industries) aim to:

1. Foster quality services
2. Support local economies
3. Promote sustainable projects

8. Production and Identity Alignment

Product development is a gateway to brand establishment. Effective promotion and distribution strategies, paired with continuous market research, ensure offerings resonate with consumer identities, fostering loyalty.

9. Capitalism with Conscience

In a capitalist framework, profitability and humanity coexist. Alioune's ecosystem balances financial goals with ethical service, targeting foundational needs—food, water, clothing, housing—while recognizing that consumer attention is today's ultimate currency.

10. Environmental Stewardship: Project NetZero

Alioune commits to planetary health, advocating for eco-friendly innovations. Project NetZero aims to deliver world-class cleaning solutions, emphasizing that environmental care is not a luxury but a necessity, even in resource-scarce contexts.

11. Emotional Intelligence: The Heart of Customer Relations

Understanding and mirroring customer emotions builds lasting connections. Monitoring feedback and refining interactions transform satisfaction into loyalty, proving that empathy is a potent business tool.

12. Conclusion: Scaling with Purpose

As Rohini Nilekani astutely notes, "What works at scale may differ from scaling what works." Alioune's journey—from pricing strategies to Afrocentric advocacy—exemplifies scaling with intentionality, ensuring��� aligns with community upliftment and planetary well-being.

5

Alioune's Vision of Business Evolution

For Alioune, evolution in business is not a linear path but a dynamic, iterative dance—one that intertwines meticulous growth measurement, unwavering accountability, and the nuanced ability to contextualize progress within ever-shifting landscapes. It is a philosophy rooted in the belief that organizations, much like living organisms, must adapt or risk obsolescence. This process demands more than quarterly reports or profit margins; it requires periodic, intentional reflection to assess not just how much a company, brand, or product has advanced, but how meaningfully it has done so. Metrics like customer lifetime value, employee engagement, and social impact become compass points, guiding strategic pivots.

Rebranding, in Alioune's view, is not a superficial facelift but a vital rite of passage. It becomes essential when an organization achieves its original vision, only to find itself at a crossroads where legacy goals no longer align with emergent realities. Consider Apple's shift from computers to lifestyle ecosystems or Netflix's evolution from DVD rentals to streaming dominance. Such transformations are not betrayals of purpose but affirmations of it—strategic refreshes that anchor the entity to its core mission while embracing new challenges.

For Alioune, this is where innovation meets integrity: a rebrand must honor the past while architecting the future.

Rebellion as a Catalyst: The Personal and the Planetary

Alioune's own journey of ecosystem evolution springs from an act of rebellion—a deliberate, almost defiant prioritization of health and well-being in a world that often equates burnout with ambition. This rebellion is both intimate and expansive. On a personal level, it manifests as daily rituals: meditation to quiet the noise, boundaries to protect energy, and a commitment to mental clarity. But this journey transcends the individual. It becomes a blueprint for harmonizing self-growth with the elevation of his interconnected ecosystem, where every entity—whether a think tank, a tribal conglomerate, or a community initiative—is a thread in a larger tapestry.

Neglect any single thread, and the entire fabric weakens. Take Fountanké Industries, his tribal conglomerate: its success hinges not just on profit margins but on how it uplifts local artisans, preserves cultural heritage, and fosters reverse mentorship. Here, rebellion against exploitative business norms becomes a quiet revolution—one that prioritizes collective advancement over cutthroat competition.

Conscience Wealth: Beyond Profit to Holistic Flourishing

Alioune's vision draws deeply from Seth Streeter's concept of conscious wealth—a paradigm where success is measured not in dollars, but in the richness of human experience. This framework integrates seven pillars:

Health: Physical vitality as the foundation of leadership.

Relationships: Collaborative networks over transactional exchanges.

Career Fulfillment: Aligning work with purpose.

Community Impact: Elevating marginalized voices.

Intellectual Growth: Continuous learning as anti-stagnation armor.

Spiritual Equilibrium: Anchoring decisions in ethical clarity.

Emotional Intelligence: Bridging logic and empathy.

Patagonia's commitment to environmental activism or Ben & Jerry's social justice campaigns exemplify this ethos. For Alioune, conscious wealth transforms businesses into custodians of well-being, where profit becomes a byproduct of purpose.

The Dual Tempo of Modern Business: Speed and Sustenance

In today's hyper-accelerated world, evolution demands a paradoxical balance: delivering instant results while nurturing long-term vision. Amazon's two-day shipping epitomizes this duality—lightning-fast service underpinned by decades of logistical innovation. Professionals now operate at speeds that would have seemed reckless a generation ago, yet Alioune argues this tempo is not inherently unsustainable. The key lies in operational alchemy: leveraging automation for efficiency, AI for predictive insights, and agile methodologies to pivot without losing strategic North Stars.

Consumer behavior has shifted irreversibly. The patience of the 1990s, when a product launch might take years, has given way to TikTok-era immediacy. Success now hinges on a company's ability to marry velocity with value—to solve problems before customers articulate them, as Uber did with ride-hailing or Duolingo with gamified learning.

Bridging Instant Gratification and Trust: The Transparency Imperative

The tension between speed and satisfaction is one of modernity's great tightropes. Alioune posits that transparency is the safety net. Real-time communication—think Shopify's live order tracking or Domino's Pizza Tracker—does more than inform; it fosters trust by demystifying processes. When Glossier crowdsourced product ideas via social media, it didn't just accelerate innovation—it built a coven of loyal advocates.

Streamlined systems, like Zara's just-in-time inventory model, ensure products integrate seamlessly into lives already stretched thin. Meanwhile, robust data monitoring—Netflix's viewer analytics, Tesla's over-the-air updates—preempts issues before they escalate. The result? A loyalty loop where speed enhances satisfaction, and satisfaction fuels retention.

The Jevons Paradox: A Cautionary Tale for Conscious Evolution

Alioune concludes with a provocation from economist William Stanley Jevons, whose 19th-century paradox warned that efficiency gains often increase resource consumption—like fuel-efficient engines leading to more driving, not less. In our era, this manifests as renewable energy tech driving up energy demand or fast fashion recycling programs justifying overproduction.

For Alioune, this paradox is a call to innovate beyond efficiency. It's not enough to make old systems less wasteful; we must reimagine them entirely. Circular economies, like IKEA's furniture buy-back program, or regenerative agriculture practices that restore ecosystems while yielding crops, point the way. True evolution, he argues, isn't about doing more with less—it's about redefining what "more" means.

In Summation: The Alchemy of Evolution

Alioune's philosophy is a mosaic of rebellion, conscience, and adaptive rigor—a reminder that businesses thrive not by chasing trends, but by architecting legacies. In a world torn between immediacy and eternity, his approach offers a compass: measure growth, but cherish purpose; move fast, but build trust; consume resources, but regenerate systems. As Jevons' shadow looms, Alioune's vision lights a path where evolution is not just survival, but stewardship.

References

1. Bodell, L. (2024, December 4). The innovation imperative: We need more time to think. Forbes.
2. Conscious wealth: How to blend purpose with prosperity. (2021, June 15). Conscious Lifestyle Magazine.
3. Hamilton, D. (2024, November 2). How to recognize unmotivated employees: Strategies to combat burnout. Forbes.
4. James, D. (n.d.). Utilizing Shohei Ohtani's goal-setting method. Entrepreneur.
5. Kotler, P., & Armstrong, G. (2023). Principles of marketing (18th ed.). Rice University.
6. Rowinski, M. (2024, December 25). Why emotional intelligence is the key to high-impact leadership. Entrepreneur.
7. Ryon, S. (2024, November 19). Ditch the "fake it until you make it" mentality. Entrepreneur.

Alioune Sow is a Senegalese entrepreneur and author who redefined resilience after incarceration, transforming adversity into innovation. Merging ancestral *sabr* (patience) with modern strategy, he champions "spiritual alchemy"—leveraging technology and cultural heritage to uplift communities. His ventures tackle digital literacy in West Africa and Afrocentric artistry, while initiatives like Project NetZero reflect his ethos of conscious capitalism. Now a mentor and strategist, Alioune advocates for purpose-driven ecosystems where profit coexists with empathy and planetary stewardship.

www.ingramcontent.com/pod-product-compliance
Lightning Source LLC
LaVergne TN
LVHW022029200926
848481LV00007B/2610
9798349211478